Rainbow

Emma Lynch

Up in the sky

It is sunny and rainy today.
Can you see a rainbow in the sky?

Rain and sun

We need rain and sun to see a rainbow.

Raindrops and sunlight make a rainbow.

Making a rainbow

As the sunlight hits the raindrops it makes a rainbow.

The sunlight bends as it hits raindrops.

The sunlight splits into seven colours.

Seven colours

These are the seven colours in a rainbow.

orange
yellow
red
green
indigo
violet
blue

A pot of gold

In an old story there is gold at the end of the rainbow.

You can keep the
gold if you find it.

The end of the rainbow

A rainbow is a
circle so it has no end!

Most rainbows are a circle. We only see half of the circle.

Find out more

Read more about the sun and the rain in ...

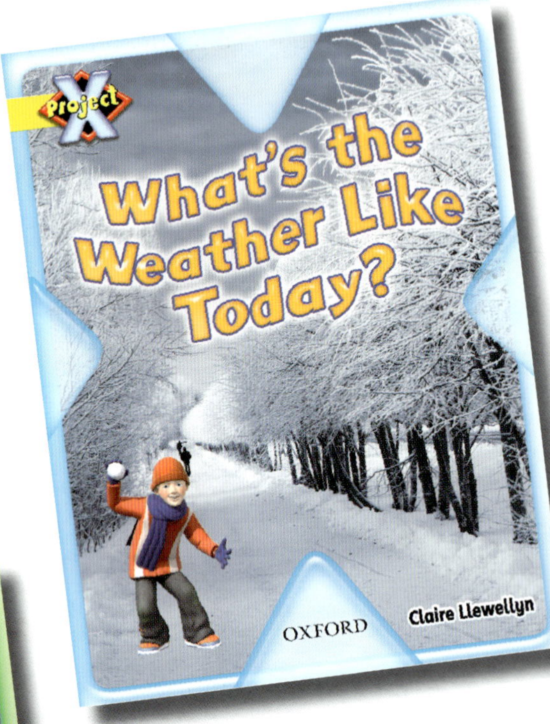

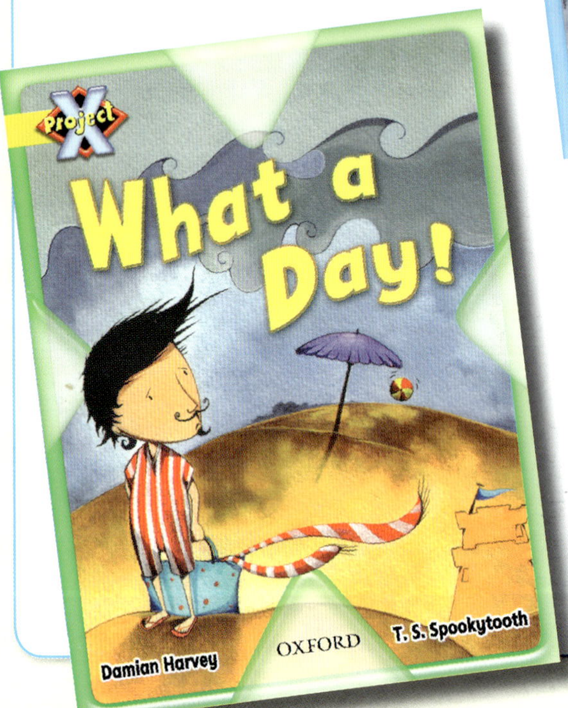

... and read about when Tizz goes to the beach.